The Storyteller

The Storyteller

The Lyrical Tales of
J. Michaels

RESOURCE *Publications* · Eugene, Oregon

THE STORYTELLER
The Lyrical Tales of J. Michaels

Copyright © 2016 J. Michaels. All rights reserved. Except for brief quotations in critical publications or reviews, no part of this book may be reproduced in any manner without prior written permission from the publisher. Write: Permissions, Wipf and Stock Publishers, 199 W. 8th Ave., Suite 3, Eugene, OR 97401.

Resource Publications
An Imprint of Wipf and Stock Publishers
199 W. 8th Ave., Suite 3
Eugene, OR 97401

www.wipfandstock.com

PAPERBACK ISBN: 978-1-5326-0214-6
HARDCOVER ISBN: 978-1-5326-0216-0
EBOOK ISBN: 978-1-5326-0215-3

Manufactured in the U.S.A.

Dedicated to those who love a good tale, yet quibble not whether penned as prose or verse, but rather let both instruct as they search for truth in the shadows of their own story

The Tales

Tale Well Spun	ix	The Demise of Mr. Hughes	53
Once Upon A Time	1	A Fragile Life	54
Nicobod & Icobod	2	Toast of the Town	55
John Henry	3	An Eagle at His Best	56
Shows to Go You	6	Tyler McShould	57
My Captain's Door	7	Nightmare for Sale	58
The Great Belgium Belch Off	9	Skinny Kid	59
Rebel Yell	11	The Journey of J Michaels	60
Man on a Wire	13	Mr. Dull & Mr. Dashing	62
Raggedy Boy	15	A Tale of Whoa	63
Jon B. Good	17	Trippin with Tom O'Leary	65
Penguard the Crusher	19	At My Papa's Side	66
Broken Truce	22	Holden Thought Aloud	67
Gridiron Hero	23	Wisdom Burn	68
She Dances Her Amens	25	On The Road to Heaven	69
Ode to Baby Michael	26	On a Good & Glorious Day	70
The Children on the Hill	27	Boy in a Cage	72
The King of Should	29	Wisdom Bone	73
Town Sheriff	30	Dead Ahead Fred & Grace	74
Hard Livin	32	The Great Cosmic Costume Ball	76
King of All	33	Alley Sage	77
The Dragon & the Old Man	34	Easy Meat	78
Ship of Dread	35	Blind Man Walking	79
No More Phantoms	36	Dr. Feelgood	80
A Complacent Man	37	Large Bromar & Smelly Smallish	81
Devoted Henchman	39	Sinister McInister	82
Searching for Sanity	40	Billy the Bully	83
A Place to Be	41	Lines of Gold	84
Poor Bobby Fischer	42	Hooker with a Heart	85
The Quest of His Dying	43	He Who Must Rhyme	86
Two Holy Men	44	Bully Meat	87
Star Man	45	His Name is Fear	88
Crown and Glory	46	My Pawpaw	89
A Most Predictable Way	48	Gradual Guy	90
The Twin Who Died	50	Peace for the Boy	91
Redemption Denied	51	Epilogue	92
Reborn Inside	52		

Tale Well Spun
(Introduction)

EVERYONE LOVES A GOOD STORY. Most enjoy a good storyteller. These are stories told in the style of the ancient storytellers, with words animated by rhythm and rhyme. They are more in the style of a Bob Dylan ballad than a Shakespearean sonnet. Such tales are woven with provocation, humor, suspense, and deep feeling, and do so without a full frontal assault. Stories, fables, parables; all leave open a host of interpretations and allow the reader to take away what he or she wants or needs or is ready to assimilate. They may teach, illuminate, or simply entertain, but a good one will most certainly pique our interest.

This medium of storytelling can convey the deepest of sorrows, the pinnacles of joy, and discover the most humane of experiences. They reveal that the greatest of human achievement often comes from the simplest of acts and that all of us involved in this mutual human experiment are far more alike than different. These are unusual tales, lyrical and haunting, attired in word and phrase. So come join us, if you will, for an excursion through the realm of mystical tales that aim to inflame your heart, provoke your mind and stir your soul. Let us once more ask the storyteller to weave us some magic and may it fill us with the wonder of the tale well spun.

Once Upon A Time

Lend me thy hearing
Fair creatures one and all
Come sit beside my fire
Let me spin tales so tall
Here in mystical forest
Among leaves and angels and such
Listen to my stories
I promise to enjoy them much
Perhaps you will too
Journey with me and see
Lands beyond our vision
Lands beyond the seas
Surpassing even the heavens
As they shine and pass away
Our humble little stories
Pass upon this day

From the poetry collection
Memories of the Future

Nicobod & Icobod

Nicobod and Icobod went up the hill
Through the valley and round the bend
They went high and they went low
They went to and they went fro
From here to there they went
Looking up and fell down
Looking for good and evil found
Searching for truth, looking for peace
Til they came upon a stone
A large obstacle in their way
They pushed and shoved
They pulled and prodded
But the stone remained
And ever will until they know
Where lives the stone
And its refrain

From the poetry collection
Common Ground

John Henry

Born a man, a proud African citizen
Taken from his home by greed and stealth
Leaving a family broken and fatherless
For money, ignorance, and greed
John Henry was strong and black
A large man, tall and imposing he stood
The body of Hercules
The soul of a dove
His family and peace were all he prized
A simple man trying to get along
Fair to his neighbors, a source for all
Living to be good, happy to be alive
Those simple sweet days gone now
As the slave traders beat and prod
Afraid of the giant, awed by his size
Yet dollars counting, they priced their prize
A gentle man captured by those less so
A tragedy born that day
Hearts broken and sadness reigned
All in a day's work and the devil's pay
John Henry wept when left alone
Too proud for the cruel captors to see
His heart heavy as his country faded
His shoreline replaced by one far away
Days of discomfort and strife
Hungry, beaten, robbed of his life
Treated as livestock, meat for sale
Reduced to headcount, his soul grew pale
The long days at sea finally passed
The new home reached at last
Uncertainty and fear his companions now
Sold to rich men, but poorer than he

John Henry

Placed on the platform for all to see
Bids placed on the man so strong
No smile for the price, no soul of the man
Body purchased and nothing more
The buyers cared not but for profit and use
The soul not of the bargain made
This gentle giant with so much to add
Stood motionless with heart so sad
Sold and purchased as merchant's wares
The property of genteel men with hearts of stone
Branded and named with no care for the man
Only muscles to them, a working machine
Life was hard, the days were long
Picking cotton in the Carolina sun
Side by side with his new family of slaves
Spirit intact and returning to life
They sang as they toiled
And spoke of days gone by
Telling stories of their homeland
And dear ones left behind
The days passed, the years quickly too
John Henry grew older and slower
No longer the machine his owners once prized
Just an old man they had come to know
The plantations thrived under John Henry's toil
Time permitted the landlords to know him well
They could not help but admire the man
Who, through the suffering and labor, stood so tall
His spirit and goodness caused them to pause
And reflect on this giant soul of a man
Even shame sought refuge
As they compared them to him
Come one fine summer day
When John Henry could arise no more
The labor and sadness taking their toll
From the man stolen so very long ago

JOHN HENRY

The master came to his bedside
To say farewell to his aged property
Humbled by one of greater character
He now cried for both souls
John Henry looked on his captor from death's door
Granting him the smile denied before
For a moment before he returned home
Brothers but for an instant
Then John Henry was no more

From the poetry collection
Common Ground

Shows to Go You

*I am reminded of a story, heard on television of all places.
I have turned it to the poet's quill and here is how it goes:*

A man waited on his rooftop
As the water rose round his home
He waited for God to rescue him
A small boat came by
And offered the man a ride
Yet he said, *No thank you
I need no place to hide*
A larger boat came roaring up
To offer the man some help
Yet he said, *No thank you
I wait for my Savior to arrive*
Soon, a helicopter flew over
And supplied the man a rope
Yet he said, *No thank you
I haven't yet given up hope*
The man drowned
And left for the pearly gates
And said, when he saw Jesus
What the hell, you were much too late!
Jesus said *what's the deal?
I sent several to delay your fate*

It just shows to go you, fixed beliefs can ruin your day.

From the poetry collection
Simple Gold

My Captain's Door

Waves are hitting hard
And tossing our ship about
The storm attacks us harshly
The fear begins to mount
The crew is less together now
Allowing fear to push apart
Maritime brothers we were
Seeming less so now
The time to pull together
Most needed in moments of peril
No other recourse given
That will save our ship of fools
And foolish we are and foolish we've been
But now the time approaches
To pull together mates
And awaken as one again
So I knock hard
Against my captain's door
Yet no reply is forthcoming
Silence answers, nothing more
Crew and ship both dissolving
Amid the tough and briny assault
Hope crashing down with the fallen mast
Only dread in common now
I call for my captain
Louder still I yell
Save us from the fate upon us
Let not our journey be to hell!
My voice finally failing
To bring the captain out
My heart and ship are breaking
Finally Heaven's name I shout

My Captain's Door

My boys pause in their terror
Knowing a divine call had been made
Leaving despair for a moment
Hoping again the storm might fade
A sailor believes in miracles
At times his only way out
Believing in man or captain
Insufficient counter to the ocean's rage
But mighty sea or thundering skies
Cower down in deference
At the call to a higher power
And make ready to obey it
The maelstrom subsided
The sea at peace again
Men's hearts calmer now
Having witnessed the divine friend
A Captain of larger stature
Who would never fail us again

From the poetry collection
Common Ground

The Great Belgium Belch Off

The crowds gathered at sunrise
To witness the annual event
The gathering of all great gas bellies
Belching here and there they went
Warming up for the day's competition
Drinking soda, beer, and air
Hoping to inflate sufficiently
And retain the belches spared
The crowds grew large and clamored for more
Of the greatest belchers Belgium had ever known
This tiny country with little claim to fame
Playing host to intestinal foam
The contest began at last
Belchers facing belchers
Under glaring spotlights
Amid frantic fans of gas
Louder and grosser the combatants became
Hours of burping took their toll
Bodies lay limp and depleted
Lesser ones belched out and spent
Those left standing all but exhausted
Until at last only two remained
The best of the belchers in Belgium land
They squared off and faced each other
Each determined to out belch the rest
Rangus McGee, the reigning champ
From the isle of green and Guinness
Facing Big George of England
Self taught at London's finest pubs
Rangus went first as custom bound
Drank his pint and held his breath
Leaving the crowd cheering and waiting

The Great Belgium Belch Off

For the inevitable blast at last
The tension mounted as Rangus held on
Face turning red as the hair on his head
The great belch on its way now
Unfettered, it roared from his mouth
Silence followed the belch supreme
The fans stunned and amazed
At what Rangus had rendered that day
A belch for the ages, leaving all dazed
Rangus now done and quite pleased
With the performance of a lifetime
Confident he had conquered
Yet another opponent less ventilated
Big George stood and hushed the crowd
His size and belly, both quite grand
He took no beverage, no aid of any kind
Simply reared back and belched his all
That left none standing, nor windows intact
Big George stood surveying the mess
That his extraordinary flatulence created
He had bested the best
Poor Rangus deflated
Defeated at last

From the poetry collection
Common Ground

Rebel Yell

Blood draining from me
Into the dirt, my bed
An unusual place to die
An unfit burial ground
It seems like so long ago
When a mere boy I was
Running through those golden fields
Riding ole Bess to school
Then one day the soldiers came
Stern faces accepting no objection
Insisting we join them or else
To defend our sovereign nation
So Daddy, Bruce, and I departed
From our beloved Carolina home
Donned the woolen grey suits
That marked us rebels all
Mama's crying, Sissy too
Left man less and defenseless
Tears in all eyes, ours too
So sad, and proud, and scared
The first day wasn't so bad
A few shots and cannons away
Still no blood flowing
No wounds to slay
By mid morning of the next
My brother lay in my arms
Nearly breathless and speechless
His life seeping away
The Lord took him that day
Bruce's blood on my sleeves
The darkness had dawned
My life would never be the same

Rebel Yell

Before the day ended
I lost my daddy too
A hole in his head, instantly dead
In one short day, three less two
From that day onward
I never really cared
If bullet or bayonet forced me
To join my men folk at Heaven's gate
At least that's where I hope we go
When I leave this world so foul
I'll tell you very shortly
Farewell, my fallen friends

From the poetry collection
Common Ground

Man on a Wire

High above the landscape
Rooftops appear below
A man looks down upon us
Makes ready to walk on air
He seems so calm, so at ease
As he stares at the depths below
What brought him here
To this time and place
Preparing to balance on wire
To walk where no one has tried
To be above the average pedestrian
To do what could only be imagined
To do what few would dare
What drives such a man
To such feats up high
Why must he do this thing
Perhaps his way to fly
Looking deep inside before the feat
To challenge both courage and means
To decide for one last time
If it is worth his death to him
For demise is what he wagers
This gamble with prize unknown
Yet something drives him to it
He obeys his chosen call
Perhaps he will know someday
What moves him to do such things
To risk his life this way
The man on a wire makes ready
The first step the hardest to take
Beyond that there is no decision
Beyond that he meets his fate

Man on a Wire

He moves to position untethered
Just him, the wire, and his pole
One step at a time is taken
Each could be his last
Like life lived well in time
He lives only in the moment
Each step defines his life
Or ends in body broken
Where he finishes at end of stride
Not his to know or even decide

From the poetry collection
Common Ground

Raggedy Boy

A street urchin born in filth
Hard times his accounting
Penniless often, all in tatters
Hungry more often than not
Begging for pennies, his trade
Resisting the call to crime
Empty pockets but soul shining bright
The street his bed, a doorway his home
Cold and hardness, his fellows
Striving each day to be a better man
While the world pressed him down
No comfort for this boy
No clothing to adorn respectable
Nothing but rags to offer cover
Nothing but darkness to hide his shame
But this man boy would never give up
Nor let the devil buy his soul
In his heart lived goodness
His mind shone bright
But try as he may
No leave granted by his life
The hard days and long nights
Brought no comfort or delight
No reason to live, no reason to fight
One rainy morn in London town
He stayed where he slept
The soul light dimming
The body now eager to die
All hope seemed lost now
No balm for his courage, all but gave out
But the day was not done
In alley so damp and dark

Raggedy Boy

Our boy had left but one request
The one thing still held dear
He longed to ask it
But no one there to hear
With nothing to lose he voiced it
A prayer departed his lips
Dear Father please grant me
This one last wish
Take this mouse from my pocket
And grant the life I give up
Be kind to this tiny creature
May he find love and a home
Not mine to grant or loan
Dear Lord, take him for your own
He died not knowing but soon discovered
The Lord always claims his own

From the poetry collection
The Poet's Quill

Jon B. Good

Jon B. Good was a rock star
Adored and cheered by many
A gift for music lived within
Treasure of his soul to share
His voice lent accompaniment
The guitar sang in perfect balance
The lyrics voiced so well
The thrill of the adventure and excitement
Flailed young Jon about
Not knowing whether coming or going
The world tilting in various ways
Pleasures and seductions surrounded
The candy store quite full
Of sundry treats and goodies
To tempt the boy to fate
Jon sang and played his tunes
To crowds who yelled and screamed
Then off to parties afterward
To numb the growing need
Young girls quite willing and available
To please and resolve the need
But bodies were not what Jon hoped for
The booze and drugs no longer worked
The emptiness that grew inside him
Not deterred by any party favor
Still he accepted the hollow offerings
Hoping enough would fill his cup
But the more he took the less he became
Knowing his life would end some day
He hoped his legacy would be
Much more than he had accumulated
More to offer for what he had become

Jon B. Good

The music his only salvation
The one pure thing he played
The only thread from soul to man
To keep Jon alive and sane
After awhile even the music dimmed
The light fading from his heart
Jon B. Good was dying
Only his body left in sight
One morning he awoke
In pool of vomit and gin
So very much to be sick about
His life reduced to this
But Jon knew he was more than this
Better than what he'd become
Something still lived within his soul
Yearning to sing its song
So Jon lifted his head and cried
The tears purifying the mess
That symbolized the life he had led
But never would again
He took his last cleansing as rock star
Alone with just his soul
Knowing his music would save him
His soul now his only muse

From the poetry collection
The Poet's Quill

Penguard the Crusher

Penguard the Crusher
A man of meager means
A hollowed out stump, his throne
He longed to be king of the Norsemen
But alas he lived all alone
Penguard the Crusher was a very large man
He stood well nigh to thirty hands
Inside he bore yet a larger heart
But life had deemed to tear it apart
His life had been filled with violence
He had savaged a man or two
His soul was chipped away with each
Yet he knew not what else to do
One day upon the path to nowhere
He encountered a tiny girl
She was lost, beaten and battered
She knew not which way to turn
In his heart he cried for the little one
It ached as he saw her pain
She reminded him of the life he lived
Had he lived it but in vain
Pen's kingly dreams would have to wait
He had someone now to protect
This lost lonely waif before him
The last thing he thought to expect
For much time the waif would not speak
Her voice had lost its tone
Then one simple act of kindness
Would remind the child of home
Old Pen held out his battle scarred hand
To offer the child some bread
She had eaten not for many a day

Penguard the Crusher

Starvation, her impending dread
The child had been left homeless
From the battles that men do wage
She had lost both father and mother
At such a tender age
Old Pen now saw those wars he'd waged
Written upon her face
Far too much for a child to know
At such a tender age
The old Norseman's heart was broken
As he looked upon the child
Knowing the life he lived
May have cast her to the wild
He had fought and pillaged for many a year
For this was all he knew
Never a boy to be remembered
Hardness and cruelty was all his due
Penguard took mercy now on this child
He would raise her as his own
He would cease the lonely warrior's life
And make them both a home
He thought what needs the child might have
He knew so little of such
He had no gold or silver
His trove was not so much
Yet he would find a way to warm her
To ease her pain somehow
He would be the lost father to her
They would be a family now
So Pen welcomed her to his home at last
It was little for the eye to see
Yet the child smiled as she entered
She had a place to be!

Penguard the Crusher

The years wore on
The girl grew strong
From the love and guiding hand
Of the old and worn out Norseman
Who had long ago left his band
To raise a child abandoned
A waif who had lost her home
He now atoned for his fruitless life
He had taken this child as his own
All those years did soften Pen's heart
The girl, he truly did love
God had granted his dream somehow
A gift from Heaven above
She attended him now as he lay in bed
Life seeping from his aged frame
She had long since forgiven
The man she had never blamed
For he had given her life
And the love of a guiltless man
She now caressed his glowing face
And she let him understand
That all he had done and committed
Was washed away by love
She then gently released him
To join his Father above

From the poetry collection
Leave the Bones

Broken Truce

Mim and Mip
Two twin sisters at three
Not too long after
They sat upon daddy's knee
One came away unscathed
The other, scarred for life
One in tenuous denial
The other in constant strife
They came of age anyway
Soon became some man's wife
And sat their child on daddy's lap
And brought their shame to life
Staring accusingly at a good man's face
Seeing it away from light
Projecting now the shame they owned
Upon a gentle man's brow
Depriving the children of trust
In the father that brought them about
Now all would suffer and die
Never seeing their brother in truth
All apart and broken they lay
With trust, the broken truce

From the poetry collection
The Fly in My Eye

Gridiron Hero

Tis an old football story
Of a gridiron warrior beyond his glory

His body was battered and broken
His heart filled with rage
No longer a viable option
To vent his anger uncaged
So he hung up his cleats
On one sad Sunday morn
He said goodbye to his team mates
All but he looked forlorn
For he was still angry
At the body that had let him down
His work, his meaning, his life
Had somehow left town
He sought for a different meaning
Something to make him whole
He found it not in wrestling
Or putting a ball in a hole
He searched somewhat frantically
For something to fill his life
He could not let in his family
His rage shut out his wife
They mourned to see his despair
This man once so proud
He seemed to be so lost now
His desperation spoke so loud
As he wandered from place to place
And then from comfort of love

Gridiron Hero

As he sought the lost meaning
He finally put on the gloves
Now as he entered the arena
And climbed aboard the ring
Facing the fighter before him
It promised a pitiful scene
In him he saw his last chance
He would face another opponent
He would accept this one last dance
The fight was short, not sweet
He barely lasted a round
Before he left his feet
Never to rise again
His life ended in defeat
Leaving a wife and children
A family now incomplete

From the poetry collection
The Fly in My Eye

She Dances Her Amens

Butterflies danced in her head
Trying to keep pace with her feet
She hardly touched down at all
She had perfected the aerial feat
Known as the loveliest of all
She was the ballerina supreme
As light as air, she was
She could dance a lightening beam
She befuddled a nearby feather
Who couldn't compete or keep up
With the lightest and loveliest ballerina
Whose dance had filled our cup
She finally alit on the floor
We had hoped it would never end
This dance that had been given
Turned out to be her amens

From the poetry collection
The Fly in My Eye

Ode to Baby Michael

Twas the day of Michael's birth
And all throughout the house
Not a murmur was intended
No meal for a delinquent mouse
He was just another boy
No legend of the south
He became quite unavoidably
The only one let out
His mother was very happy
His father was quite proud
They welcomed new baby Michael
And heard him say out loud
That he wasn't so happy to be here
He'd rather been left uncrowned
Yet he joined the human race
The one that no one wins
He's planning on doing his best
In the hopes we can all begin
To see what lies before us
The joy behind the veil
To invite and accept the unusual
And wait for sweet love to prevail

From the poetry collection
The Fly in My Eye

The Children on the Hill

One day in eternal bliss
Some children played at will
Reveling in their innocence
Knowing all was well
They played atop a grassy knoll
It was lush and emerald green
They frolicked in the sunshine
Knowing all to be seen
Wise beyond recognition
Holy through and through
Innocence in children form
Playing two by two
An errant thought did enter
Mind so pure and fair
One they forgot to laugh at
And led them away from there
A wish to leave the fold
A desire to be one of all
Leaving the tender oneness
Of all in one recalled
So leave, they did
These now orphaned souls
Departing from oneness once known
To dream in hell's murky hole
In darkness they sought their way
Hoping to find light again
And illuminate a place to pray
Regret and guilt guide them now
As they seek a sacrificial way
Paying at any cost

The Children on the Hill

For transgressions of mind betrayed
Yet they know not what they do
For they are lost and blown away
At last from afar
A lantern light is seen
Labeled love, they were told
A hope for souls redeemed
They reached the light at last
First a few then many more
Guided by God's Holy Spirit
They arrived where they were before
Instant rejoicing came upon them
Now knowing the whys and wherefores
Back in the greener pastures
Playing in innocence once more

From the poetry collection
The Best of Times

The King of Should

There once lived a King of Should
A land long put aside
Known as a non frivolous place
A place where could would hide
The king was quite the ruler
He had a rule or two
He was the King of Should
Telling his subjects what to do
He had a list of items
Some things they all need know
Some laws and rules to live by
Axioms to clearly show
That only the king knew better
That he alone was king
And therefore follow his rules they should
And see what that will bring
I'm betting the king will suffer
In his efforts to be quite fair
For rules are made for kings
And not for those who care
About justice, love, and sharing
And for brothers who need our care

From the poetry collection
The Best of Times

Town Sheriff

I lived a time or two ago
Wore the sheriff's badge
Walked those dirty streets
A gun was all I had
I never wanted to use it
Dealer of death on my hip
I never wanted to kill a man
Nor see blood upon his lips
For awhile it stay holstered
I talked a good game I guess
Til the day the gunslinger came
A day I will soon confess
Die or kill my brother
This was the choice of mine
I was ready for neither
Nor a box made of pine
I knew fate faced me
As I stared at eyes so cold
Did he want my death
Or to steal my soul
I refused to draw first
I told him to make up his mind
Kill, die, or walk away
Please, I thought, don't stay
I witnessed the eyes as they changed
From hate to fear to none
I touched my brother that day
With peace between us, seen as one

Town Sheriff

A miracle in that dusty street
Enough killing was our plea
It was time to live in peace
It was time to simply let be

From the poetry collection
Heaven Revisited

Hard Livin

Hard livin
I've done my share
Rode it long and hard
Nothing or no one spared
The fast lane
Drove it for awhile
Sped past most everything
Missed them by a mile
Caught up in pleasure
No notice of the pain
Kept on going at it
Again and again
Used a lot of people
Including as well myself
Gobbled it all up
Put my soul on the shelf
Too busy getting my rocks off
Too absorbed in little ole me
Blazing through the details
That brought me to my knees
Hard livin done it to me

From the poetry collection
One In The Same

King of All

How could I ask for more
When I thought I had it all
Yet one day I did
It precipitated my fall
I said to my Father
Father, give me more
He smiled and gently replied
My son, there is no more
Still, I wanted to know
If I could be king of all
I whispered to my brothers
Come, let us leave the All
They asked me why, in surprise
They could not believe their ears
Why would they leave the All
For something which promised tears
Oh, but to be king, I replied
Of all this and more
Yet I knew not the truth
That All was the more
So journey we did, to hell
Nothing for All, the deal
I still don't know why I did it
I hope to soon repeal
All that I gave up
In an impossible sort of deal
When you have it all
There is nothing left to steal

From the poetry collection
A Merry Bunch of Folly

The Dragon & the Old Man

The dragon offers mastery
In the tail he holds at bay
Heart as pure as diamond
Born to ever stay
He addresses the old man
With tale and fable told
Beckons him to play
Upon his flute of splendid gold
Play me a jig, old man
Let happy be our way
Touch my heart with your music
Let my spirit play
The old man smiles
To hear of innocence this way
Gladly he lifts his flute
And upon it starts to play
The notes which issue forth
From instrument held in hand
Uniting the hearts of both
Dragon and ancient man

From the poetry collection
A Merry Bunch of Folly

Ship of Dread

A likely pirate ship
Painting horizon's view
Flying the skull and bones
Sailing straight and true
Waves breaking before the bough
Afraid to do any less
The ship of death approaches
Bringing foul and blackened breath
Fear precedes its coming
Dread precedes promised death
Sail away, The captain commands
Flee before it arrives
Let courage not desert us
Let it save our mortal lives
Hurry mates, it comes near
Row harder for your life
All we have is gold
To give to please their strife
As they come upon us
For I fear that end is near
Stow the fruitless gold
In a place both near and dear
Perhaps to pay the reaper
As the ship of dread draws near
I pray they take our gold
And leave our lives intact
To sail again tomorrow
And take a different tact
To sails towards the sunrise
Towards our homes, in fact

From the poetry collection
No More Silly Mistakes

No More Phantoms

He was a drunken sot
Simply going through the motions
Not caring to live or die
He felt no great emotions
The world to him was bleak
Darkness was his fold
Death, strangely attractive
Dare he lie dead and cold
He thought this to himself
As he placed the gun to his head
Was it worth the effort
To kill that already dead
Then a tiny whisper
Coming through the dark
A tiny ray of light
A slightly glowing spark
An ember about to fade
From his drunken heart
Til he named it hope
And blew his world apart
No blood that day was let
Only illusion lost its day
He laid down his costly flagon
Went down a different way
His ember did glow some more
Soon it turned to light
No more drunken stupors
No more phantoms to fight

From the poetry collection
A Universe of One

A Complacent Man

He never caused a ripple
He never bucked a trend
He was most acceptable
He was a reasonable man
He never questioned authority
Never rocked the boat
Never challenged an assumption
Lived his life by rote
He seemed barely alive at times
He wasn't sure what to do
He lived his life unquestioned
He barely had a clue
It seemed a bit rocky
Boring at times as well
It never seemed fulfilling
It seemed a bit like hell
But at least he fit right in
He never caused a stir
With this he was complacent
To let it all occur
Then one day he arose
A day like any other
Though he still fit in
He longed now for his brother
And in that waking instant
He knew he had been alone
Trapped in his obeisance
To a life lived as clone
Just like all the others
Who seemed so quite alone

A Complacent Man

He knew now his complacency
Had kept him from his home
Not the one he lived in
Not a box and street
But the one housed in brotherhood
The one he had failed to reach
He longed to go beyond
The normality of his life
To reach out to his brother
Beyond the usual strife
He saw now no reason
To maintain such a dismal day
He chose now to be open
To a non complacent way

From the poetry collection
Futility Dream

Devoted Henchman

A devoted henchman
The priest turned out to be
Frozen by belief
In a vision he could not see
Yet he suffered no lack of direction
He knew exactly where to go
He had no doubt whatsoever
The good book told him so
You see he took it literally
Even those meant to show
That literal doesn't help us
When there's so much more to know
He was trapped like a dogma
Imprisoned in a perceptual pen
Locked up tight by doctrine
Hoping to avoid his sin
His voyage ended fruitless
For he never found that sought
He failed to let words point
To where, in truth, they ought

From the poetry collection
Heaven Revisited

Searching for Sanity

He seems to be searching
This man I witness now
Perhaps he's come unhinged
Lost his mind somehow
He wanders from branch to bough
Seeking somewhere to find
A tidbit of pure sanity
Something to save his mind
Maybe it's too late
He seems quite detached
From what of him is expected
He still has wonder to catch
He glides among the field
Floating here and there
Perhaps he's found some sanity
Yet still not sure of where

From the poetry collection
Heaven Revisited

A Place to Be

There once was a man quite homeless
He lived in car and tent
He paid no living expenses
Pride, his only rent
Yet he lacked in faith at the time
Allowing fear to seep in
Retaining it for years to come
Treasuring it as his sin
Afraid to fully confront it
Reluctant to face his fear
Til all became his suffering
Til the fear became too near
Soon he faced once again
The prospect of no home
The fear would not forget
How he had felt so all alone
Yet to be whole again
This, his princely fee
For just beyond his fear
A place to set him free
A place to simply be

From the poetry collection
Futility Dream

Poor Bobby Fischer

Poor Bobby Fischer
Lived too much in his head
Got lost in the intellect
Until he turned up dead
He saw the insanity
Living inside his head
Put it all on the world
Should have looked inside instead
The insanity he saw
Was likely there in seed
Yet once he lost his enemies
He knew not how to proceed
I see it too
In the world at large
Yet Love persuades me
Of its superior charge
It keeps me safe
Through minefields of the mind
Poor Bobby Fischer
Was not so inclined
He lived long alone
Stuck inside his head
Until he wandered lost
Until he turned up dead

From the poetry collection
Futility Dream

The Quest of His Dying

The cup fell from his hand
In the wee hours of dawn
Causing quite the stir
In a life lived as pawn
He clutched his chest
As the pain seared
He knew the end had come
As he had long since feared
In a brief elongated moment
He thought of where he'd been
He pondered on the purpose
Of a life committed to sin
For long had he believed
That all was guilty as he
Now in this briefest of moments
His mind was allowed to see
The perfection of it all
The innocence of fellow man
It took the quest of his dying
To make him understand

From the poetry collection
Heaven Revisited

Two Holy Men

Two holy men were lowered into a pit by an evil captor. The pit was deep, dark, and had the stench of death. There had been stated but one condition, one way for the holy men to escape. *Only one may live!* The holy men agree, of course, to let God decide who should live and who should die. The first to perish from starvation or thirst would prepare a place in Heaven for his noble hearted brother. They would let fate determine their course.

The evil captor waited patiently. He believed that, as hunger and thirst set in, the foreboding fear would arrive and perform its dastardly deed. One would eventually turn on the other and take his so called *brother*'s life.

The two holy men soon faced impending deaths as their thirst threatened to choke off their lives. They both now truly faced extinction. One found it to be dark and threatening, the other saw light and freedom. Neither was certain of his plight. The thought soon crossed both minds that perhaps they were the one who should live. After all, why should both perish; the likely outcome if nothing was done.

Why should this other "brother" be the one to live. He seems shifty to me. I'll wager he has foul intent. Perhaps I should strike first, land the decisive blow. If so, fate would surely ally itself with me and the greater man would survive. God will have spoken through my raised and clenched fist!

The deadly fear threatened consumption of both souls, the minds having already given themselves over to its sway. As one brother turned away to reconsider, the other raised his arm to slay. At the very last instant, the brother turned to face what he knew in his heart was his death. He raised his eyes to those of his brother and through their darkness, love came into play. Through their eyes this was conveyed. From then on, neither would be slayed, the captor assuaged by what two holy men had portrayed.

From the poetry collection
Heaven Revisited

Star Man

The star man searched the universe
Looking for a likely Whole
He found a lack of space
From a hole someone stole
He rode from star to star
A galaxy done in a day
Looking for that place
Where he could lonely stay
He traveled far and wide
Kept looking into space
Searching for a solution
For what he inevitability faced
He found his Self at last
He never found a place
He discovered the key to eternity
There, in a state of grace

From the poetry collection
Guilt Free, To Be or Not to Be

Crown and Glory

Listen now to a tale of olde
A long and fabled story
Of a brave and valiant knight
Who gave all for crown and glory
Stout of frame
Soft of heart
Skilled as warrior
Unable to impart
How he felt
Or what he thought true
A subordinated will
Was all he ever knew
He pledged unfailing loyalty
Heart and mind, he gave away
To serve his king on Earth
To himself, he gave no sway
His life was short and lonely
This life he did not own
Given to counterfeit king
Whom he mistook for his own
He denied himself completely
Servant, through and through
Living for another
To himself he remained untrue
To battle he rode away
To defend the honor of king
Glory was his recompense
No honor did it bring
He took many a life
In defense of a counterfeit thing

Crown and Glory

He should have turned within
Focused on a higher King
The one who gave him life
The only authentic thing
His new King asked him now
For the killing to be no more
To spare the lives his blade may claim
For the counterfeit king he served no more

From the poetry collection
Guilt Free, To Be or Not to Be

A Most Predictable Way

A jaded gangster
His son destined too
Subject to a life
Unfit for the true
The boy went along
One day at his insistence
To watch his father at work
To watch him earn subsistence
The father thought to prepare him
For what life would send his way
Without the possibility
That he could walk away
For as he would soon see
No one leaves a life like this
Once you embrace the darkness
It will not cease or desist
So on this day of journey
The boy would see too much
He would witness his father at work
Committing murder and such
He knew his father now
In a way he wished he hadn't
For now his mind was broken
His young heart so very saddened
The innocent was less so now
A child soon brought about
To see what no boy should see
And to know of no way out
He would be insisted to stay
Otherwise he was liability

A Most Predictable Way

If he tried to go
They'd extinguish his viability
Sadly, he chose his weapon
Knowing what it well meant
He now was so intended
To do for what he was sent
The first time he pulled the trigger
And watched another man die
Something died in him
The lad inside did cry
Yet the man holding the gun
Had set his fate in stone
He could no longer face his God
He believed he was all alone
The day his father died
In hail of bullets blind
He felt no lonely dispatch
He had left his soul behind
He grew his reputation
Much as his father had
By the killing of his brothers
Then condemning his soul as bad
He felt hollow and not worth living
He saw no salvation ahead
He could only see his father
And all they had left dead
So he pulled out his revolver
And put it to his head
And ended his life that day
In a most predictable way

From the poetry collection
Guilt Free, To Be or Not to Be

The Twin Who Died

The mother lay spent upon the table
Giving birth to twins this day
One of them survived it
The other went away
Not long after
Husband by her side
Both in deep despair
For the twin who had died
There was little joy that day
For the boy who did survive
His tiny brother dead and gone
Half of him had died
The boy grew tall and gaunt
Sadness always at his side
With parents who never forgot
The identical twin that died
His life, a constant reminder
Of the missing part inside
Peace eluded all three
Forgiveness never replied

From the poetry collection
Guilt Free, To Be or Not to Be

Redemption Denied

As the twin grew to manhood
He sought his mother's grace
Yet every time he approached her
He saw only shame on her face
He searched her eyes for forgiveness
For he had blamed himself
Yet all he saw was guilt
All else she kept to herself
He had hoped for a note of redemption
So he could forgive his own
Yet still she denied it to him
Her heart remained as stone
She could not love her son
Without recalling his twin
She could not forgive herself
She could not release her sin
So her son she kept at bay
Until soon he moved away
She had lost another son
As she had on that terrible day

From the poetry collection
Guilt Free, To Be or Not to Be

Reborn Inside

Life was hard for the man/boy
He never spoke of his twin
He never mentioned his mother
Or how he bore her sin
One day he met a woman
Who reminded of one he knew
Perhaps he could find redemption
If her love was true
They courted, loved, and wed
And soon she was with child
His heart was much confused
His mind would soon run wild
He thought of his future child
And hoped he would father well
He prayed his lovely bride
Would deliver him from his hell
The day drew near for the birth
The twin was much confused
Until his bride bore two
His heart no longer refused
To love them as he longed to
To give what he was denied
Loving and forgiving
The twin who had long since died

From the poetry collection
Guilt Free, To Be or Not to Be

The Demise of Mr. Hughes

There's no understanding Mr. Hughes
He's crazy as a loon
Perhaps they'll tell his story
In a movie coming soon
He lived too much in the world
Should have invested in his soul
He bought so many pieces
That failed to make him whole
Now he's come apart
Tearing at the seams
Insanity in full command
Whatever his ego deems
Too bad for the world
So sad for Mr. Hughes
A genius lost so soon
He's blown a mental fuse
There's just no understanding
The demise of Mr. Hughes

From the poetry collection
Guilt Free, To Be or Not to Be

A Fragile Life

This story I am telling
Must visit in my head
It comes from tale not mine
This came to me instead
It comes from my father
And he is long since dead
My mother told the tale
Of a night on lonely road
When an aged man stepped forth
Onto that driven road
My father saw too late
Car and body did explode
The old man died
A part of my dad as well
None his stolen fault
Still he went through hell
Taking another's life
Right or wrong it be
Changes the lonely life taker
Alters the way he sees
Life appears more fragile
Than ever thought to be

From the poetry collection
Hiding From the Dark

Toast of the Town

A once famous actor
Feature of the stage
Fallen on hard times
A victim of his rage
Formerly quite popular
The toast of the town
Then he lost his temper
The anger brought him down
Now he hands out ice cream
From the rear of an ice cream truck
Signing autographs unwanted
His ego seems quite stuck
To them he's just an old man
With a frown upon his face
Still so very pissed off
Still bitter about his fate
He has a chance to learn
Something he needs know
Will he stay in rage
Or will he seek to know
That beauty is not skin deep
It lives only in our soul

From the poetry collection
Hiding From the Dark

An Eagle at His Best

There once flew an eagle
Who soared to heights unknown
His need moved him upward
Seeking his long lost home
He searched the sky without end
Eventually to return to nest
Back where he had started
Where he had been his best
There he felt quite lost
He had not found that sought
And as he gazed to the clouds
He missed what he ought not
There all around him
In that warming nest
Were all who had loved him
There he was at his best
The eagle that had soared
Found the home he sought
There in that humble nest
Was the home love had wrought

From the poetry collection
Hiding From the Dark

Tyler McShould

Old Tyler McShould
He was a proper old man
He had lived by regulation
Never took a stand
He saw truth
Passing him by
Yet he maintained as he should
He turned a passive eye
He thought maybe he should
Look deeper at his lot
Perhaps his mind was constricted
Perhaps it had turned to rot
He was a bit tired of pretending
That all was all right with him
He suffered a lack of absurdity
Straight laced, from stern to stem
When he finished his life
They laid him out quite straight
All those conforming years
Made him unable to relate
To the living and the thinking
So he might as well just die
For without a mind to guide him
Life had passed him by

From the poetry collection
Revenue Streams

Nightmare for Sale

Welcome to my nightmare!
He screamed as curtain rose
All who sought to follow
Now in frightened repose
Welcome to hell, companions
Join me in my mind
See if you like the scenery
Of a darkened kind
The audience soon awakened
To what his offer meant
To join him in his darkness
To watch his soul dement
To gather all around him
Despite his dubious intent
Come on in and see me
He beckoned to the throng
No need to worry, my friends
How can you go wrong
Lest his siren song
Lead you far astray
Bend your mind towards light
And never look away
Tell him to keep his show
Tell him you refuse to pay

From the poetry collection
Hiding From the Dark

Skinny Kid

Once upon a time
Lived a skinny kid
Geeky and silent
Rarely opened his lid
Got his rail ass kicked
Many a day or two
Got over it eventually
He learned a thing or two
He got smart about the world
Learned to play its games
Got along quite well, he did
Yet all appeared inane
So he looked inside for answers
He looked from whence he came
He wanted no more the world
It seemed to him insane
Then one day he sought it
That missing piece of him
Hidden deep within
The chances were quite slim
He looked within and found nothing
That looked the least like him
And though he could not see it
He felt it all around
And though he could not hear it
He had no need of sound
And though he could not touch it
He knew he had been found

From the poetry collection
Welcome World

The Journey of J Michaels

The journey of J Michaels
Has long been that of joy
Pain perhaps did accompany
That quiet little boy
A life quite enigmatic
Stretched at many a point
Caught up in the action
Thought he'd smoke a joint
Much has come and gone
Much has stayed inside
Banished many a demon
Took it all in stride
Yes, both highs and lows
Some deep and dark places
Always there was hope
That he would win his races
Once he crossed the line
They told him he was finished
He found it empty and wanting
His soul was not replenished
He searched for many a day
Long nights were his friends
He liked too much the victim
He let no one in
One day a time did come
When he saw beyond his grief
Climbed out of his sadness
Assumed a better belief
He tasted love, my friends

The Journey of J Michaels

The One that rings so true
He saw in his Beloved
There, both me and you
It changed his life forever
This simple joyous thing
He no longer held his sadness
His heart was free to sing
And sing he did, this boy
After all those years of pain
He felt at long long last
That now he was quite sane
Yet the journey has not ended
He has some things to do
He awaits his Beloved's instruction
To show him what is true

From the poetry collection
Welcome World

Mr. Dull & Mr. Dashing

A glimmer from the darkness
Brought this story to light
Of two very different people
Both who thought they were right
Roommates, turns out, they were
Though of differing sorts
One ran long and hard
The other lounged long in shorts
One thought it better outward
The other, the inward choice
One fought for better conditions
The other silenced his voice
One worked hard to make things easy
He feared no such walls
Mr. Dull fought no battles
He heard no rallying calls
Mr. Dashing could not agree
With the other part of he
Dull was not his choice
Of whom he'd rather be
They both took different paths
The goal the same, free to be

From the poetry collection
A Universe of One

A Tale of Whoa

Don't stop me if you've heard this
Tis a tale of woe
A story of two farmers
And a mule that wouldn't hoe
Said one farmer to the other
Lend me that mule you own
I have a present need
For my seed to be sown
The farmer smiled a smile
And said, *Of course, my friend*
Let me fetch that mule
And home with you I'll send
The farmer thanked him gladly
And shook so well his hand
Thank you for the mule
I can use an extra hand
All was well between them
Or at least so it seemed
Until the farmer returned
With the mule and much displeased
Said the farmer to his friend
Why so soon returned
Did not he serve you well
And give your soil a turn
The farmer felt quite sad
This gift he did return
Yet told his friendly friend
It would not mind or learn
The farmer then issued a smile

A Tale of Whoa

And said, *I know the fault*
Let me take it from you
And make this behavior halt
The farmer was quite grateful
But soon he was surprised
The other friend, his farmer
Hit the mule between the eyes
He then laid down the beam
That had met the donkey's head
He said then to his farmer friend
I don't think he's dead
You just need get his attention
And clear his head instead

From the poetry collection
A Universe of One

Trippin with Tom O'Leary

Old Jim McCreary
Met up with Tim O'Leary
They ate a pill and took a trip
And boy it got quite scary
Things got so distorted
He thought he might be whack
The landscape looked so different
He thought he might not get back
That pill, it opened doors
That he never knew existed
It pulled him through a portal
Though he greatly resisted
He no longer knew real from false
What was true and what was lie
It opened up his mind
And it nearly passed him by

From the poetry collection
Memories of the Future

At My Papa's Side

I yearn to see a time
From the times gone bye
I yearn for the warmth
At my papa's side
Twas a pale dawning
That day I dressed up
To visit once more my papa
As he lay dressed and stuffed
I knew it wasn't him
That lay before me now
As I relive that moment
That returned to me somehow
I could summon no tears
That day at coffin side
I just knew he was gone
I wanted only to hide
Remembering those walks
As we journeyed to the store
Walking by his side
And then, never more

From the poetry collection
Memories of the Future

Holden Thought Aloud

Unify and simplify
Holden thought aloud
Didn't make much sense to him
It didn't make him proud
His mind had wandered much
Separate and complicate, his creed
He seemed a bit deranged
His soul seemed in need
He's toying with insanity
Coming apart at the seams
Losing his grip on reality
Grasping at any means
What the hell's going on
Fuck you in every scene
He's got some problems
That's obvious and clear
Who knows where he ends up
And if he leaves his fear
Will he ever see clearly
With that inner eye
Is he catching any body
A coming through the rye

From the poetry collection
Memories of the Future

Wisdom Burn

He went trying to find a fuck
A place to lay his eggs
A place to bury his hatchet
While getting a little laid
He didn't give a shit
About where he came to roost
As long as he got his rocks off
And gave his ego a boost
The women were just there
Something for his use
He knew only self satisfaction
And not his sister's abuse
For when he took too much
And yes that day did come
He felt so very empty
Nobody loved him some
He saw that all he had taken
With so little given in return
Now came back to haunt him
As he started the wisdom burn
Soon he would see himself
In quite unflattering terms
And yet to turn to ash
As he suffered the wisdom burn

From the poetry collection
Memories of the Future

On The Road to Heaven

Upon the road to Heaven
I met an elder man
He spoke to me in mime
I did not understand
Yet he spoke with such kindness
He sounded unlike a man
I asked if he knew
The way to Heaven's Door
He pointed to my heart
And said nothing more

From the poetry collection
Memories of the Future

On a Good & Glorious Day

The old man ambled
On his way across the street
Humbled and bent, he was
He shuffled his tired old feet
I saw in him as I watched
The man I was soon to be
Body disappearing
Barely able to hear or see
It seemed to me quite pitiful
A threadbare dignity he wore
Yet I saw in him released
All the life gone before
He held no long forgottens
He retained no days gone by
All youthful glory surrendered
All need had left his eye
As I watched him walk
So slowly in front of me
I saw his spirit waiting
To see what it would be
A tear demanded passage
My heart did open wide
Seeing his physical suffering
Body worn, no comfort abides
As he passed barely by
He turned his head to me
He smiled the wisest smile
That I did ever see

On a Good & Glorious Day

His gentle manner disarmed me
I saw my brother there
In body worn and humbled
Becoming as light as air
I knew now what he meant
In eyes that said so much
That he was but passing
To a place of kinder touch
He knew, I could see it
In his wise old eyes
As if he knew his future
Held a sacred prize
He looked at me as if to say
I'll see you when we get there
On a good and glorious day

Boy in a Cage

There's a child in the cage
Who yearns to come and play
Who wants only joy
Who lives for today
I am the boy's jailer
The keeper of the keys
Keeping the child caged
Failing to set him free
Fear of joyful play
Has been my prior way
Afraid to let him out
Unable to have his say
The boy cowers in the corner
In fear of what awaits
Not knowing how to love
Not knowing who to hate
Though I open the door
And beckon the boy arise
Fear still restrains him
I can see it in his eyes
The past he does reprise

From the poetry collection
The Other Side of Letting Go

Wisdom Bone

The eagle soars
And sings once more
About a desperado
Knocking at his door
A lonely lonely man
Afraid of being alone
Asks boon of the eagle
To toss him a wisdom bone
The eagle laughs
And says, *my friend*
The sky is my home
You've come to yours end
How may I explain
To such a lonely man
The nature of his freedom
Is hard to understand
The desperado weeps
His life is at an end
The eagle simply smiles
Knowing here, he will begin

From the poetry collection
The Other Side of Letting Go

Dead Ahead Fred & Grace

Dead ahead Fred
Was quite an ordinary guy
Charging blindly forward
And not really knowing why
He seemed quite focused
Determination at its best
Willing his way forward
Ever at the quest
When he got done
With all that doing
He had nowhere left to go
He had given himself a screwing
As he sat dejected
Head down in his hands
Completely at a loss
And failing to understand
That all that pointless doing
Was no longer in demand
He fell into despair
He knew not what to do
Until he saw sweet Grace
And what she brought as true
Quite the vision she was
Ethereal and feather light
She showed him his Being
And where to find the light
He tried so much to hold her
Doing all that he could do

Dead Ahead Fred & Grace

Yet the tighter he clung
The more she slipped through
As quietly as she came
She left without a clue
Leaving only clarity
And nothing left to do

From the poetry collection
A White Rose on a Dark Night

The Great Cosmic Costume Ball

All great beings gather
Once a millennia or so
All dressed up in finery
Only one place left to go
It's the greatest ball of all
A spectacular cosmic event
Donning the best of costume
You can buy or rent
Form in manifestation
Countless modes of variety
Stretching imagination
Hoping for notoriety
On the far side of the galaxy
They meet in glorious form
Dancing upon the stars
The impossible is the norm
All will surely know
The very grandest of times
Celebrating Divine Creation
All in perfect time

From the poetry collection
A White Rose on a Dark Night

Alley Sage

To some, just a bum
To others, a true friend
The sage of the alley
Wise without end
Dealing daily with despair
Souls were at stake
The unloved and unwanted
Whom no one else would take
To him, they were quite precious
Children of God, he saw
Souls crying for help
Hearts that knew no flaw
Living lives most simple
Survival was all they knew
Living another moment
Knowing there were but few
Bearing the deepest of pain
Suffering so few knew
To these he did minister
On these he spent his love
The sage of the alley
Speaking wisdom from above
Calling Home the least of these
All in the name of Love

From the poetry collection
A White Rose on a Dark Night

Easy Meat

There he stood
The shy kid in the hood
Easy prey for villains
So well they understood
Easy Meat, they called him
They meant to pick him clean
Leaving only bones
Not even dignity
All it took
Was one short look
To see the mark of Cain
On him it was mistook
They saw him as retribution
For what they suffered so
A punching bag of indifference
To relieve their tortured souls
For what they did to him
Was done to them before
They simply wanted revenge
And to close that dreaded door
To be easy meat no more

From the poetry collection
Pedro's Intrigue

Blind Man Walking

Once upon a time
A blind man walked the earth
Not knowing he was blind
Was his daily curse
Stumbling here, falling there
Making lots of mistakes
Some called it sin
Most can relate
So it is we ask ourselves
Who would do such a thing
To send a blind man walking
On such a silly fling
What must be the purpose
For such a tortuous toil
What is it he sought
From what did he recoil
His fate quite simple
Right before his eyes
Learning he was blind
To living so many lies

From the poetry collection
A Whole New Point of View

Dr. Feelgood

Ole Doc Feelgood
He's helping young Bill O'Day
Whipping out the pill pad
Selling a happy day
Chasing the blues away
Ole Doc Feelgood
He's forgotten how to heal
If ever he did know
What was pill and what was real
Things have gotten so easy
The dollars keep rolling in
Doc keeps writing prescriptions
The healing never begins
He doctors all those symptoms
He never looks within

From the poetry collection
A Whole New Point of View

Large Bromar & Smelly Smallish
(An Unlikely Love Story)

A quite unlikely pair
One looms so large
The other cannot compare
Large Bromar, they call him
Smelly Smallish, her tag
He's a bit huge
She's a small bag
She's diminutive, smelly, and old
Yet Bromar loves her still
He sees her inner beauty
He know he always will
Large is quite the hulk
Yet tiny Smelly doesn't care
For each other they are perfect
Love is in the air

From the poetry collection
A Whole New Point of View

Sinister McInister

Ole Rod McInister
Was quite the sinister soul
Scheming and conniving
Divisive to the whole
He never knew what drove him
To be so mean and cruel
He seemed to be so driven
To be the soulless fool
Honesty in life eluded
A place to call his home
Destined to keep conniving
In his most sinister tone
He longed for love lost
To fill his empty soul
Something to breach his loneliness
Something to make him whole

From the poetry collection
A Whole New Point of View

Billy the Bully

Willy, Nilly, and Silly
Three siblings quite content
Until brother Billy came
And brought with him dissent
Silly was never serious
Willy and Nilly ran amok
Billy pissed them all off
He never gave a fuck
For Billy was a bully
The rest were out of luck

From the poetry collection
Pedro's Intrigue

Lines of Gold

For seven years he wrote
Line upon line of joy
Ciphering what was given
For all dear hearts to enjoy
Twas a labor of love indeed
Blessings beyond number
Turning a morning's phrase
Waking us from our slumber
Telling stories upon stories
To stir the heart and soul
Lessons to be learned, my friends
All to make us whole
He cried, he laughed, he paused
As the stories did unfold
Listening with open heart
To tales so sweetly told
Blessed to be the messenger
Delivering lines of gold

From the poetry collection
Pedro's Intrigue

Hooker with a Heart

Good ole Lena from Pasadena
A happy hooker from day one
Offering her goods for sale
Disguised as sex and fun
Yet to Lena it mattered not
This was the life she had
She sought to find the good
In the role that all thought bad
She saw a lot of shit
Life was hellish at times
Yet in its hellish grip
She found that sought to find
She had the gift of love
This prostitute was all heart
Though life was hard to live
She knew this was but part
Determined to make the best of it
This hooker with a heart

From the poetry collection
Pedro's Intrigue

He Who Must Rhyme

At first, a simple silliness
Arose within his mind
It nagged and them it tempted him
What if he only rhymed
At first, it was a trickle
An accident of words
Until what issued forth
Seemed so similar heard
At first, it did amuse
Tickled his fancy too
It seemed whatever he said
Included a rhyme or two
At last, to himself, he said
I must relinquish my time
It seems it just ran out
But finished with a rhyme

From the poetry collection
Pedro's Intrigue

Bully Meat

When I was but a kid
Small, introverted, and shy
I seemed to attract the bad
They couldn't pass me by
Somewhere on my being
Labeled me a fool
Bullies seemed to like me
They liked to be so cruel
I labeled myself a coward
For fear of being harmed
I had no natural defenses
I had no way to disarm
So I cowered before them
Paid them their putrid due
Took their humiliations
Trying to just get through
I survived, I did
It even made me strong
Discovered all that I was
Discovered I was not wrong
Bully meat no more
Fear no more my song

From the poetry collection
Pedro's Intrigue

His Name is Fear

To a dark and troubled soul
This mystery appeared
Moving in the shadows
Just as some had feared
Like a fleeting vapor
He floated through the air
A black and smoky flavor
Warned he was there
Voices vaguely heard
Following a vacant trail
Faint screams in the distance
Suggesting sounds from hell
He stole into town that night
Like a thief in the dark
Leaving trails of sorrow
Stripping beauty to the bark
His name was fear
The underside of the arc

From the poetry collection
Pedro's Intrigue

My Pawpaw

When I was but a boy
Holding my pawpaw's cane
Walking in loving trust
Oblivious to pending pain
The best times of my life
In southern comfort found
By my pawpaw's side
His protection all around
A loving gramma
Awaited our daily return
Surrounded by her love
There I could always turn
Then that loving place
Of warmth and protection found
Died that horrible day
When they laid my pawpaw down
I turned to my gramma's love
As I saw her fleeting face
Crying for such loss
As we left that loving place
A parody of Heaven
Traded for a hellish space

From the poetry collection
Pedro's Intrigue

Gradual Guy

He's a gradual guy
He likes to inch ahead
Moving ever so slowly
Hell, he could be dead
Throwing caution to the wind
Is not the way he goes
Oh so very carefully
Avoiding careless woes
Danger has little appeal
Safety is his way
The only chances he takes
Are guaranteed to pay
He seldom gets the highs
In avoiding all those lows
Straight down the middle
Is how this tortoise goes

From the poetry collection
Pedro's Intrigue

Peace for the Boy

Violence hung in the air
Above the words of hate
Anger thick among them
The boy could not relate
Attack and attack back
Rage filled the room
Hurtful words and images
Paint a scene of doom
The boy is filled with fear
He feels so all alone
Two of three in anger
Taking pain to the bone
He knows not what to do
Defenseless and remote
Fading further from reality
Trying to simply cope
Then one day, a baby
A brother for the boy
Someone now for him
A loving one to enjoy
The screaming now diminished
Some peace now for the boy

From the poetry collection
Pedro's Intrigue

Epilogue

I hope these tales did satisfy and refused to let you be complacent. Whether they have stirred your soul or touched your pain, I pray they have at least reached you in some way. As you have seen, they represent the gamut of human foible and folly and show us much about ourselves. They also point to the atrocities of the world and the pain they cause us all.

Whether they made you laugh or cry, feel pain or joy, at least they made you feel. Some say there are only two true emotions, love and fear. Our emotional lives would seem to distil down to those two if we look long and hard at the core issues that afflict and enliven us. Yet, even if true, I would speculate that although love stands alone as our saving grace, fear subsumes and brings with it a host of siblings such as guilt, hate, and greed.

Let's face it; the world we live in is a hard and oftentimes cruel place to be. Not all of us experience the full force of its brutality, like the *Raggedy Boy* or *Penguard's* waif, but we may at least know someone who has. We all will experience its final outcome of death, perhaps preceded by pain and suffering. Yet even within this difficult and pitiless place, we find glimmers of hope. We bear witness to the black giant who, despite having the humiliation of enslavement imposed upon him, rises above his captors and leaves them with an example of true humanity and forgiveness. We are inspired by the old warrior who lays down his sword and shield to provide a loving home for a homeless child. And we see, amidst the perils of the angry sea, courage and faith save the day.

These are stories, above all else, of love and hope. They are precursors and prophesy of what life here haunts us with and what a life of love and redemption offers as alternative.

www.ingramcontent.com/pod-product-compliance
Lightning Source LLC
Chambersburg PA
CBHW070307100426
42743CB00011B/2380